Introduction

Luscious cold desserts, created from fresh ingredients are always a success and throughout this book there are delicious confections made from fruit, ice cream, jelly, chocolate, yogurt, cream and sponge fingers. Many of the recipes are subtly spiced or include favourite ingredients such as vanilla, coconut, lemon rind, mint, cherries and nuts. There are recipes suitable for all members of the family, plus a selection of more sophisticated desserts with entertaining in mind.

Recipe Notes

All spoon measures are level: 1 tablespoon = 15ml spoon; 1 teaspoon = 5ml spoon.

Follow EITHER metric or Imperial measures and NEVER mix in one recipe as they are not interchangeable.

Eggs used are a medium size 3 unless otherwise stated.

For additional hints and tips on segmenting oranges, filling and using a piping bag and beating egg whites, see step-by-step instructions and pictures on pages 18-19.

Kilojoules and kilocalories at the end of each recipe are represented by the letters kj and kcal.

This edition published 1994 by Merehurst Limited
Ferry House, 51-57 Lacy Road,
Putney, London SW15 1PR
Copyright © Gräfe und Unzer GmbH 1991, Munich
ISBN 1 87456 36 0
All rights reserved
Designed by Clive Dorman & Co.
Printed in Italy by G. Canale & C.S.p.A
Distributed in the UK by J.B. Fairfax Press Limited,
9 Trinity Centre, Park Farm, Wellingborough,
Northants NN8 6ZB
Distributed in Australia by J.B. Fairfax Press Pty Ltd,
80 McLachlan Avenue, Rushcutters Bay,
Sydney, NSW 2011

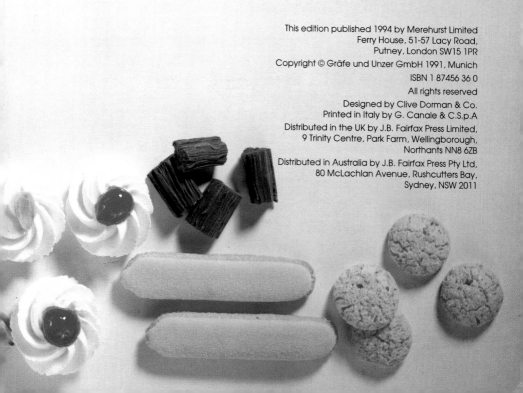

Berry Pudding with Snow Balls

Serves 4

A brilliantly coloured mix of fresh berries, decorated with snow balls made from beaten egg whites.

Preparation time: about 40 minutes
Cooking time: 15 minutes
Cooling time: 1½-2hours

750g (1½ lb) mixed fresh berries including
   stoned red cherries
155ml (5fl oz/⅔ cup) red wine or apple juice
3 tablespoons caster sugar

SNOW BALLS
4 egg whites
Dash of lemon juice
2 tablespoons caster sugar
2 litres (3½ pints/8 cups) water

1 Rinse fruit gently under cold running water and leave in colander to drain.

2 Bring wine or apple juice and sugar to the boil in a large shallow saucepan, stirring frequently.

3 Add fruit to saucepan and poach, uncovered, over low heat for 5 minutes. Switch heat off and leave pan on hob until fruit has cooled. If fruit seems to be lacking in juice, add 2 or 3 tablespoons water. Transfer to bowl, cover and chill.

4 To make snow balls, beat egg whites with squeeze of lemon until stiff. Gradually beat in sugar and continue to whisk until whites become thick and glossy.

5 Bring water to a gentle boil in large shallow saucepan. Drop in tablespoon of egg white mixture and cook for about 10 seconds, turning snow ball over after this time. The egg white should float to top of water. Repeat process with remaining egg whites cooking no more than six snow balls at a time.

6 Lift snow balls out of pan with draining spoon and put on to folded tea towel to drain. Serve straight away on top of fruit.

Nutritional value per portion:
about 740kj/175kcal
Protein: 6g
Fat: 1g
Carbohydrate: 30g

Berry Pudding with Snow Balls

Peach Melba

Serves 4

Quick and easy to prepare, this dish is one of the great French classics.

Preparation time: about 50 minutes

4 or 8 canned peach halves, depending on
  size

RASPBERRY SAUCE
440g (14oz) fresh or frozen raspberries
125g (4oz) icing sugar
4 tablespoons water
1 teaspoon vanilla essence
1½ teaspoons arrowroot
3 teaspoon water
1 teaspoon lemon juice
2 tablespoons Kirsch or Cointreau

TO SERVE
250g (8oz) vanilla ice cream
75ml (2½ fl oz/⅓ cup) whipping cream,
  whipped until thick

1 Drain peaches on absorbent kitchen paper and set aside.

2 To make sauce, put raspberries, icing sugar and 4tablespoon water into saucepan and slowly bring to the boil. Reduce heat and simmer, uncovered, for 3 minutes. Remove pan from heat and stir in vanilla essence.

3 Rub sauce through fine sieve directly into a clean saucepan. Blend arrowroot with water and lemon juice until smooth, then stir into raspberry sauce in pan.

4 Bring sauce to the boil, lower heat and simmer until sauce comes to the boil and thickens, stirring constantly. Simmer sauce for 1 minute then cool to luke warm. Stir in liqueur, cover and set aside until completely cold.

5 To assemble, put peach halves on to 4 plates with slices of ice cream. Surround with raspberry sauce and pipe a whirl of cream on to each.

Nutritional value per portion:
about 1300kj/310kcal
Protein: 4g
Fat: 7g
Carbohydrate: 57g

Peach Melba

Fruit Salad with Yogurt Sauce

Serves 4

This refreshing fruit salad makes an excellent starter or dessert.

Preparation time: about 30 minutes

1 medium Ogen melon
2 kiwi fruit
250g (8oz) strawberries
1 tablespoon lemon juice

DRESSING

2 tablespoons clear honey
155g (5oz) natural yogurt
1 teaspoon lemon juice
10 lemon balm or mint leaves

1 Halve melon and remove seeds. Using melon baller or teaspoon, scoop flesh into large bowl.

2 Peel kiwi fruit, halve lengthwise and cut each half into thin slices.

3 Rinse strawberries and slice or halve depending on size. Add kiwi fruit, straw-berries and lemon juice to melon in bowl.

4 For dressing, combine honey, yogurt and lemon juice.

5 Spoon fruit salad into dishes, top with yogurt dressing and decorate with lemon balm leaves.

TIPS

Use raspberries instead of strawberries and orange slices instead of kiwi fruit.
If liked, add125g (4oz) seedless green grapes to the fruit salad.

Nutritional value per portion:
about 525kj/125kcal
Protein: 3g
Fat: 2g
Carbohydrate: 24g

Fruit Salad with Yogurt Sauce

Chocolate Mousse

Serves 4

One of the most popular desserts of all time.

Preparation time: about 40 minutes
Setting time: 3 hours

125g (4oz) plain (dark) chocolate
15g (½ oz) butter
3 eggs, at room temperature
4 tablespoons icing sugar, sifted
Dash of lemon juice
155ml (5 fl oz/⅔ cup) whipping cream

1 Break up chocolate and put into bowl set over saucepan of gently simmering water. Add butter and stir until melted.

2 Separate eggs into two bowls.

3 Add half the sugar to egg yolks and beat until thick and creamy. Gradually beat into melted chocolate. Remove bowl from saucepan.

4 Whisk egg whites until stiff. Gradually whisk in remaining sugar and continue whisking until mixture is thick, glossy and stands in firm peaks when beaters are lifted.

5 Using a large metal spoon, fold egg whites gently into chocolate mixture.

6 Whip cream until thick then gradually fold into chocolate mixture.

7 When mixture is smooth and evenly-combined, transfer to 4 individual serving dishes. Chill for about 3 hours or until set.

TIP
You can flavour the mousse to taste with coffee essence or alcohol by adding it to the chocolate and butter as it melts.

Nutritional value per portion:
about 1355kj/325kcal
Protein: 6g
Fat: 24g
Carbohydrate: 22g

Chocolate Mousse

Strawberry Blancmange with Advocaat

Serves 4

Strawberry blancmange with a touch of sophistication.

paration time: about 20 minutes
Standing time: 4 hours

1 packet strawberry blancmange powder
375ml (12fl oz/1½ cups) cold milk
1 tablespoon redcurrant jelly, melted
2 tablespoons caster sugar
155g (5oz) crème fraîche
Extra caster sugar
4 tablespoons advocaat or egg flip

1 Empty packet of blancmange powder into small bowl. Add a little of the milk and mix to a smooth thin paste, stirring briskly with wooden spoon.

2 Pour into saucepan and add remaining milk, redcurrant jelly and caster sugar.

3 Cook until blancmange comes to the boil and thickens, stirring constantly.

4 Simmer for 1 minute over a low heat then gradually add crème fraîche.

5 Rinse 4 individual fancy moulds or 1 large one with cold water. Fill with blancmange then sprinkle top with a little sugar to prevent a skin forming. Cool, cover and chill for 3 hours or until set.

6 Unmould blancmange on to serving plate and spoon over advocaat.

TIPS

1 Lightly sweetened single cream may be poured over blancmange instead of the advocaat.
2 If you have no fancy moulds, set in glass dessert dishes or wine glasses and do not turn out.

Nutritional value per portion:
about 1020kj/245kcal
Protein: 9g
Fat: 3g
Carbohydrate: 41g

Strawberry Blancmange with Advocaat

Easy Lemon Mousse Ring

Serves 4

A perfect summer dessert.

Preparation time: about 40 minutes
Standing time: 4-6 hours

1 packet lemon flavour jelly
2 eggs
Finely grated rind of 1 medium lemon
2 tablespoons lemon juice
2 tablespoons caster sugar
155ml (5fl oz/⅔ cup) whipping cream

DECORATION
2tablespoon chopped citron peel,
    crystallised ginger or angelica

1 Divide jelly into cubes and put into measuring jug. Make up to 440ml (14fl oz/1¾ cups) with boiling water and stir until melted. Alternatively, melt jelly with water in a saucepan over low heat.

2 Cool jelly, cover and chill until just beginning to thicken. The consistency should be like that of unbeaten egg whites.

3 Separate eggs. Beat egg yolks into setting jelly with lemon rind and juice.

4 Beat egg whites until stiff then gradually whisk in 1 tablespoon sugar and continue beating until mixture is thick, glossy and stands in firm peaks when beaters are lifted. Whip cream separately until thick.

5 Using a large metal spoon dipped in warm water, fold cream and beaten egg whites alternately into lemon jelly mixture until smooth and well combined.

6 Spoon mousse into wetted jelly ring mould, cover and chill for 4-6 hours until set. Unmould mousse on to serving plate and decorate with citron peel, ginger or angelica.

Nutritional value per portion:
about 1285kj/305kcal
Protein: 7g
Fat: 15g
Carbohydrate: 37g

Easy Lemon Mousse Ring

Tutti Frutti Salad with Vanilla Sauce

Serves 4

A colourful dish of summer fruits served with a smooth vanilla sauce.

Preparation time: about 45 minutes

6 large ripe apricots
250g (8oz) red cherries
1 dessert apple
1 tablespoon lemon juice
1 tablespoon clear honey

VANILLA SAUCE
1 egg
1 teaspoon vanilla essence
1 tablespoon caster sugar
1 tablespoon cornflour
1 tablespoon cold water
315ml (10fl oz/1⅓ cups) milk
1 chocolate flake bar

1 Wash apricots and wipe dry with absorbent kitchen paper. Halve and remove stones. Cut flesh into slices and put into mixing bowl.

2 Wash cherries and remove stones. Add to bowl with apricots.

3 Peel, quarter and core apple and cut flesh into small pieces. Add to bowl of apricots and cherries then stir in lemon juice and honey. Cover and set aside.

4 Separate egg, putting white into bowl and yolk into saucepan.

5 Stand saucepan over low heat then beat in vanilla essence and sugar. Blend cornflour with cold water until smooth then stir into pan and whisk until foamy. Gradually beat in milk.

6 Cook sauce until egg yolk mixture comes to the boil and thickens, stirring constantly. Simmer for 1 minute then remove pan from heat.

7 Whisk egg white until stiff and fold into sauce with large metal spoon.

8 Divide fruit salad equally between 4 dishes. Top with sauce and add 2 pieces of chocolate flake bar to each.

Nutritional value per portion:
about 920kj/220kcal
Protein: 5g
Fat: 5g
Carbohydrate: 38g

Tutti Frutti Salad with Vanilla Sauce

STEP-BY-STEP
Preparing Orange or Grapefruit Segments

1 Peel orange or grapefruit, removing all traces of white pith.

2 Hold whole fruit in one hand and, using sharp knife, cut out fruit segments from in between tough membranes.

3 Each segment should be in one piece, free from pith and membrane.

1

Filling and Using a Piping Bag

4 Fit star-shaped or plain tube inside plastic, cloth or paper piping bag. The size of tube can be small, medium or large according to type of decoration required.

5 Stand piping bag inside glass or jug for support. Fold back top of bag over rim of glass or jug. Spoon in cream.

6 Lift up top of bag and twist tightly just above mixture inside. Pipe by squeezing bag. Refer to piped decorations inside back cover.

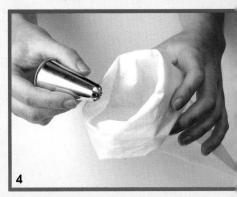
4

Making Meringues

7 Separate the eggs into a large, clean, grease-free bowl, making sure that none of the egg yolk gets into the white.

8 Whisk the whites with a pinch of salt using electric beaters until the whites are stiff and dry when the beaters are removed.

9 Whisk in the sugar, a spoonful at a time. Whisk well between each addition to make a stiff, shiny meringue.

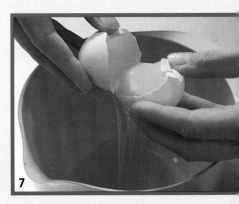
7

2

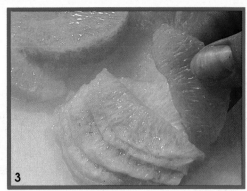

3

5

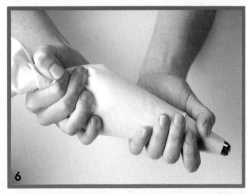

6

8

9

Tiramisu

Serves 4

A new version of a great Italian invention. The name means tonic or pick-me-up.

Preparation time: about 30 minutes
Cooling time: 3 hours

2 eggs
60g (2oz) caster sugar
Pinch of salt
220g (7oz) Italian Mascarpone cheese, at
    room temperature
280ml (9fl oz/1 cup) cold espresso, made
    from instant coffee and water
16 sponge finger biscuits

DECORATION
Cocoa powder

1 Separate eggs, putting whites into one bowl and yolks into another.

2 Add sugar to yolks and beat until thick, creamy and very pale in colour.

3 Put Mascarpone cheese in a bowl and mix in egg yolk mixture. Whisk egg whites with salt until stiff, then fold into cheese and egg mixture with large metal spoon.

4 Pour coffee into shallow dish. Cut 8 sponge fingers in half and dip briefly into coffee until soft on outside but still firm in middle.

5 Arrange coffee-soaked sponge fingers over base of shallow dish and cover smoothly with half the cheese mixture.

6 Halve remaining sponge fingers as before and arrange on top of cheese.

7 Spoon remaining cheese on top and dust with sifted cocoa powder.

TIP
Flavour Mascarpone mixture with 2 tablespoons rum or brandy.

Nutritional value per portion:
about 1405kj/335kcal
Protein: 11g
Fat: 20g
Carbohydrate: 26g

Tiramisu

Raspberry Blancmange Pudding

Serves 4

Children will love this deep pink blancmange pudding.

Preparation time: about 40 minutes
Standing time: 4 hours

1 packet raspberry blancmange powder
315ml (10fl oz/1¼ cups) cold milk
2 tablespoons caster sugar
1 tablespoon blackcurrant syrup
155g (5oz) natural yogurt
2 eggs

DECORATION
Slices of fresh or canned fruit
1teaspoon chopped pistachio nuts or
    walnuts

1 Empty packet of blancmange powder
into a bowl. Add a little of the cold
water and mix to a thin, smooth paste. Add
remaining milk.

2 Pour into saucepan and add sugar and
syrup. Bring to the boil, stirring
constantly, then simmer for 1 minute until
thick. Remove pan from heat and gradually
beat in yogurt.

3 Separate eggs and beat yolks into hot
blancmange.

4 Whisk egg whites until stiff and fold into
blancmange with a large metal spoon.

5 Spoon blancmange in to wetted
pudding bowl or 4 individual bowls.
Sprinkle tops with sugar to prevent a skin
forming then cool and cover.

6 Chill blancmange for 4 hours until set.
Turn out and decorate with fruit and
chopped nuts.

TIP
If preferred, set blancmange mixture in individual dessert dishes and do not turn out.

Nutritional value per portion:
about 395kj/95kcal
Protein: 5g
Fat: 3g
Carbohydrate: 12g

Raspberry Blancmange Pudding

Double Chocolate Pudding with Cream

Serves 4

An irresistible chocolate blancmange, perfect for entertaining.

Preparation time: about 25 minutes
Standing time: 4 hours

1 packet chocolate blancmange powder
560ml (18 fl oz/ 2¼ cups) single (light) cream
2 tablespoons caster sugar
90g (3oz) plain (dark) chocolate, grated
½ teaspoon vanilla essence
1 egg

DECORATION
155ml (5fl oz/⅔ cup) whipping cream
1 tablespoon chopped pistachio nuts
Ratafia biscuits (optional)

1 Empty packet of blancmange powder into bowl. Mix in a little of the cream to form a smooth paste, then stir in remainder.

2 Pour into saucepan and cook until mixture comes to the boil and thickens, stirring. Simmer for 1 minute.

3 Remove pan from heat and add sugar and grated chocolate. Stir until both have melted. Add vanilla essence.

4 Separate egg and beat yolk into hot chocolate blancmange mixture.

5 Whisk egg white until stiff then fold into blancmange with large metal spoon until smooth and well combined.

6 Spoon blancmange in to wetted fancy mould. Cool, cover and chill for 4 hours until set.

7 Unmould on to a serving plate. Whip cream until thick, pipe a border around edge of blancmange and sprinkle with nuts. Pipe swirl of cream in the centre and top with a ratafia if liked.

Nutritional value per portion:
about 1750kj/415kcal
Protein: 8g
Fat: 23g
Carbohydrate: 45g

Double Chocolate Pudding with Cream

Russian Lemon Cream

Serves 4

A luscious lemon flavoured dessert.

Preparation time: about 30 minutes
Standing time: 4 hours

410g (13oz) sweetened and skimmed
  condensed milk
220g (70z) crème fraîche
Finely grated rind and juice of 2 medium
  lemons
2 egg whites
1 tablespoon caster sugar

DECORATION
1 medium lemon
Mint leaves

1 Spoon condensed milk into mixing
bowl and gradually beat in crème
fraîche, grated lemon rind and juice. Stir
thoroughly until well combined.

2 Whisk egg whites until stiff. Gradually
add sugar and continue whisking until
mixture is glossy and stands in firm peaks
when beaters are lifted.

3 Using a large metal spoon, fold egg
whites gently and lightly into
condensed milk and lemon mixture.

4 Spoon mousse into 4 dishes and chill for
4 hours.

5 Thinly slice lemon and use to decorate
mousses with mint leaves.

TIPS
1 Use lime slices instead of lemon to decorate.
2 1-2 tablespoons of orange flower water,
added with the lemon rind and juice, gives
the dessert a slightly exotic and perfumed
flavour.

Nutritional value per portion:
about 1310kj/310kcal
Protein: 8g
Fat: 16g
Carbohydrate: 27g

Russian Lemon Cream

Pears Hélène

Serves 4

Quick and easy to prepare, this classic dessert makes an ideal midweek dessert.

Preparation time: about 20 minutes
Cooking time: 10 minutes

8 canned pear halves in syrup
2 tablespoons pear syrup from can
1 tablespoon water
½ teaspoon vanilla essence
125g (4oz) plain (dark) chocolate
155ml (5fl oz/⅔ cup) whipping cream
8 slices vanilla ice cream

1 Drain pears thoroughly on absorbent kitchen paper.

2 To make sauce, pour syrup into heavy-based saucepan. Add water and vanilla essence. Break in chocolate.

3 Cook over moderate heat until chocolate has melted, stirring frequently. Cool.

4 Whip cream until thick then gradually add cooled chocolate sauce.

5 Arrange pears and ice cream on 4 plates.

6 Spoon over chocolate sauce and serve straight away.

Nutritional value per person:
about 2060kj/490kcal
Protein: 6g
Fat: 27g
Carbohydrate: 46g

Pears Hélène

Vanilla Fluff with Fruit

Serves 4

Light and airy, this dessert makes a perfect end to a heavy meal.

Preparation time: about 30 minutes

750g (1½ lb) firm strawberries
2 eggs
4 tablespoons caster sugar
500g (1lb) fromage frais or skimmed milk soft
  cheese
Pinch of salt
155ml (5fl oz/⅔ cup) whipping cream
1 teaspoon vanilla essence
Grated rind and juice of 1 small orange
45g (1½ oz) chopped hazelnuts

1 Hull strawberries, tip into colander and wash gently under cold running water. Drain thoroughly. Reserve a quarter of the strawberries and slice remainder.

2 Separate eggs, putting yolks into one bowl and whites into another.

3 Add 3 tablespoons sugar to egg yolks and beat until thick, foamy and pale in colour. Gradually beat fromage frais or soft cheese into egg yolks.

4 Whisk egg whites with pinch of salt until stiff. Gradually add remaining tablespoon of sugar and continue whisking until mixture is thick, glossy and stands in firm peaks when beaters are lifted.

5 Using a large metal spoon, fold egg whites into fromage frais mixture alternately with strawberries.

6 Whip cream until thick. Stir in vanilla essence and orange juice and fold into fromage frais mixture.

7 Spoon into serving dish and sprinkle with orange rind. Decorate with nuts and remaining strawberries.

Nutritional value per portion:
about 1700kj/400kcal
Protein: 24g
Fat: 22g
Carbohydrate: 26g

Vanilla Fluff with Fruit

Redcurrant and Fruit Cake Dessert

Serves 4

Redcurrants are combined with rich fruit cake in this simple-to-make dessert.

Preparation time: about 50 minutes
Standing time: 1½ hours

500g (1lb) redcurrants
90ml (3fl oz/⅓ cup) water
125g (4oz) caster sugar
250g (8oz) rich dark fruit cake
1 tablespoon rum
155ml (5fl oz/⅔ cup) whipping cream
250g (8oz) fromage frais or skimmed milk soft
   cheese
4 tablespoons icing sugar, sifted
1 chocolate flake bar

1 Wash redcurrants, remove stalks and put three-quarters of the fruit into a saucepan.

2 Add water, bring to the boil then lower heat and cover. Simmer gently for 10 minutes or until currants are soft.

3 Add sugar to currants and stir until dissolved. Crumble cake into small pieces and add to fruit in saucepan. Leave to stand for 30 minutes then stir in rum.

4 Transfer to serving dish. Cover and chill for 30 minutes.

5 Meanwhile, whip cream until thick then combine with fromage frais or soft cheese.

6 Sweeten with icing sugar and spoon over top of pudding

7 Arrange remaining redcurrants around edge of pudding then decorate with pieces of flake bar.

8 Chill for a further 30 minutes then spoon on to plates to serve.

Nutritional value per portion:
about 2005kj/480kcal
Protein: 21g
Fat: 11g
Carbohydrate: 67g

Redcurrant and Fruit Cake Dessert